Renewals

0333 370 4700

arena.yourlondonlibrary.net/
web/bromley

Please return/renew this item
by the last date shown.
Books may also be renewed by
phone and Internet.

Celebrate Spring
Animals in Spring

by Kathryn Clay

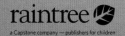

a Capstone company — publishers for children

Raintree is an imprint of Capstone Global Library Limited, a company incorporated in England and Wales having its registered office at 264 Banbury Road, Oxford, OX2 7DY – Registered company number: 6695582

www.raintree.co.uk
myorders@raintree.co.uk

Edited by Erika L. Shores
Designed by Juliette Peters and Ashlee Suker
Picture research by Svetlana Zhurkin
Production by Katy LaVigne
Originated by Capstone Global Library
Printed and bound in China.

ISBN 978 1 4747 1235 4

19 18 17 16 15
10 9 8 7 6 5 4 3 2 1

British Library Cataloguing in Publication Data
A full catalogue record for this book is available from the British Library.

Acknowledgements
We would like to thank the following for permission to reproduce photographs: Dreamstime: Saje, 13; iStockphoto: MRaust, 19; Shutterstock: AEPhotographic, 7, bluecrayola, 11 (inset), Cindy Underwood, 1, Dennis van de Water, 9, Edwin Butter, cover, Gucio_55, 17, Jiang Hongyan, 3, Kletr, 5, Matt Jeppson, 21, Matteo Photos, 11, Menno Schaefer, 15, USBFCO, back cover and throughout, Vasily Vishnevskiy, 7 (inset).

Every effort has been made to contact copyright holders of material reproduced in this book. Any omissions will be rectified in subsequent printings if notice is given to the publisher.

All the internet addresses (URLs) given in this book were valid at the time of going to press. However, due to the dynamic nature of the internet, some addresses may have changed, or sites may have changed or ceased to exist since publication. While the author and publisher regret any inconvenience this may cause readers, no responsibility for any such changes can be accepted by either the author or the publisher.

Contents

Spring is here!

Animals are busy in spring.

They build nests.

They find food.

Babies are born

A duck finds twigs and leaves.

She makes a nest for her eggs.

Soon ducklings waddle.

They splash in ponds.

Frogs lay eggs.

Tadpoles hatch.

They grow into adult frogs.

Rabbits make grass nests.

Baby rabbits cuddle.

Fox cubs yip.

Mothers bring back food.

Sleepy animals wake up

Bats stretch their wings.

They look for food at night.

Bears leave their dens.
They find plants to eat.

Snakes lie on rocks.

The sun warms their bodies.

What do you do in spring?

Glossary

den animal home

hatch break out of an egg

nest home made by an animal for its young

tadpole life stage between egg and frog

Find out more

Mammal Babies (Animal Babies), Catherine Veitch (Raintree, 2013)

Rabbit's Spring Adventure, Anita Loughrey (QED, 2013)

What Can You See in Spring? (Seasons), Sian Smith (Raintree, 2014)

Websites

www.bbc.co.uk/education/clips/z7kc87h
Find out how the changing seasons affect hedgehogs.

kids.nationalgeographic.com/animals/
Find out more about animals on this website.

www.squizzes.com/who-hibernates
Learn about animals that hibernate.

Index